DATE DUE

N W

THE WORLD OF MUSIC

EDITED BY SIR GEORGE FRANCKENSTEIN, G.C.V.O., AND OTTO ERICH DEUTSCH

ITALIAN OPERA

GIUDITTA PASTA IN ROSSINI'S 'SEMIRAMIDE'. WATER-COLOUR BY A. E. CHALON, ·1828

FRANCIS TOYE

ITALIAN OPERA

With 40 Illustrations

LONDON

MAX PARRISH & CO LIMITED

FIRST PUBLISHED 1952 BY

MAX PARRISH AND CO LIMITED ADPRINT HOUSE RATHBONE PLACE LONDON W.1

IN ASSOCIATION WITH

ADPRINT LIMITED LONDON

PRINTED IN GREAT BRITAIN BY
CLARKE AND SHERWELL LTD NORTHAMPTON

CONTENTS

ILLUSTRATIONS

ILLUSTRATIONS

The Editors' thanks are due to Edward Croft-Murray, Esq., and to the Raymond Mander and Joe Mitchenson Theatre Collection for their co-operation in providing some of the pictures in this book.

To

NANCIE TOWLE

AN 'INTERMEZZO' (TEXT BY RINUCCINI). FLORENCE, 1589
Stage design by Bernardo Buontalenti delle Girandole

I

L'INCORONAZIONE DI MONTEVERDI

IT is often stated in text-books that opera began with the production
in the year 1600 of a work called *Euridice*, a dramatic poem by Rinuccini
set to music by Jacopo Peri. As a general and useful simplification this
statement can stand, but a few reservations are necessary.

To begin with, in the year 1600 there was no such thing as "opera"; the
term was not invented till the middle of the century. Secondly, the famous
controversial work by Vincenzo Galilei, illustrious father of a still more
illustrious son, from which sprang directly the revolutionary ideas destined
to result in what we call opera, had in fact appeared some twenty years
earlier. Lastly, there had been attempts in several directions to unite music
and poetry for dramatic purposes many years before the famous meetings
in the house of Count Bardi of the Florentine amateurs to whom the credit
of the new invention is, as a rule, exclusively ascribed.

Who were these amateurs and what did they think they were doing?
Aristocratic intellectuals, they were literary men rather than musicians,

9

though Peri enjoyed a considerable reputation as a singer. Rinuccini was an established poet, and all of them were interested in music, however limited their skill in writing it. The main object they had in view was to create something to correspond to the old Greek play (in which of course music played a considerable part) and to use music solely to heighten the meaning and expressiveness of words. Anticipating Wagner, they called this new form *dramma per musica*. The impression on a modern listener would be one of long continuous recitative. Before *Euridice* their first experiment was *Dafne*, with music, now lost, by Peri and others.

These performances were not public. They were designed for private parties in the houses of the great and, as in the English masque, spectacle played a very important part. They were essentially aristocratic entertainments, designed to gratify the tastes of a fashionable public bored with polyphony and counterpoint.

But for a fortunate accident it may be doubted whether anything permanent would have come of these experiments because, whatever their general aesthetic qualifications, Peri, Caccini and Co. were the veriest amateurs as compared with the masters of the school they had set out to supersede. This accident was the accession to their cause of Claudio Monteverdi. Born in 1567 at Cremona, the son of a doctor, Monteverdi was a musical genius of the first order with the benefit, moreover, of a thorough schooling in the art. Not only that; he was a remarkably independent and adventurous character. Even in the madrigals written in his youth he had not been afraid to experiment with dissonances that aroused the ire of the traditionalists, if he thought the effectiveness of the musical setting of the words could thereby be enhanced. He knew and liked French music even if he himself remained wholly Italian.

It is not surprising that Monteverdi, whose genius lay first and foremost in the expression of human emotion, should have been attracted by the new theories of the Florentine amateurs. The Florentines were in reality only interested in words and viewed music but as a means of heightening their expressiveness. Naturally a musician so accomplished by nature and training as Monteverdi could never unreservedly accept such a position; for him music remained at the very least an equal partner, and when, in 1607, he first had the chance of putting his theories into practice he produced what was immediately recognized as the masterpiece of the New Music: *Orfeo*, the setting of a tragedy by Striggio. Not only was his recitative far more free and plastic than that of his predecessors in the genre but he made use of his long experience as a madrigalist to write many delightful choruses and

PROLOGO
LA TRAGEDIA.

PERI'S 'EURIDICE'
Detail of the score published in 1600/1

ballets. The Duke of Mantua, typical Renaissance potentate that he was, saw to it that his Court was well supplied not only with singers but with an adequate number of instrumentalists, and all these resources were placed at Monteverdi's disposal for *Orfeo*. At the time it was unanimously voted the most successful entertainment of the kind hitherto known, and even today the extraordinary poignancy of some of the music stands out, though it remains impossible for us to reproduce the conditions—especially the instrumental conditions—in which it was originally given.

Orfeo was followed a year later by *Arianna*, written for another even more important court function. *Arianna* seems to have been conceived on the same lines as *Orfeo* but the music has disappeared with one notable exception. This is the famous "Lasciatemi morire", the only piece by which Monteverdi is conceivably known to the average member of the modern public. Almost at once, it evoked the admiration of the aristocracy of the whole peninsula; it was arranged for every kind of combination and later was even turned into

MONTEVERDI'S 'ORFEO'
Title-page of the 1615 edition

a madrigal by Monteverdi himself. Since it is one of the most heart-rending expressions of grief ever translated into music this is not surprising. People have said that it reflected the despair of Monteverdi at the death of his much-loved young wife; it is certainly representative of the quality that makes Monteverdi one of the greatest European musicians.

In 1613 Monteverdi was appointed Master of Music to the Venetian Republic. Beyond question this was a step up. At Venice his salary was far higher and, what is more, he was officially the dictator of all Venetian music, whether secular or ecclesiastical. He was very happy in his new surroundings, and it is worth noting that one of the first acts of this erstwhile revolutionary was to restore the pure tradition of *a cappella* singing in the Cathedral. During the thirty years spent in Venice he wrote a very large quantity of music of every kind, but most of it unfortunately is lost.

Fortunately however among the survivals are the two scores that he wrote for the newly-opened public opera theatres in Venice: the *Ritorno d'Ulisse* for the Teatro San Cassiano and the *Incoronazione di Poppea* for the Teatro di SS. Giovanni e Paolo. This opening of opera to the public, which first took place in 1637 in Venice, is of capital importance in that it tended to change the fundamental aesthetics of the form. Quite apart from the fact that the taste of the public, not that of a highly sophisticated aristocracy, was henceforward to determine the success or failure of an opera, the technical resources of the public theatres were decidedly inferior to those found at the courts of princes; for instance there was nothing like the same number of instruments or of chorus singers.

Consummate craftsman that he was, Monteverdi, when writing for the public theatres, made no bones about adapting his style to the changed material at his disposal, as can be seen by the difference between the music he occasionally still wrote for private pageants and the music he wrote for the public theatres. *Il Ritorno d'Ulisse* (1641) need not detain us; *L'Incoronazione* (1642) on the other hand is perhaps the most important work that Monteverdi ever wrote. Comparison between it and *Orfeo* is revelatory indeed. The recitative is once again far more plastic, with a marked tendency throughout to the *arioso*. Whereas in the first operas the characters had almost necessarily to be legendary or semi-divine, the Emperor Nero and his wife Poppaea are here the protagonists. Not only that; there are even a few comic scenes by way of contrast with the noble grandiloquence of Seneca and other high Roman personages. Such concerted music as there is was provided not by a chorus, but by the characters themselves. Monteverdi produced this exceptionally vital and glowing score in his middle seventies, and a year later, on the 29th of November 1643, he died, the acknowledged doyen of Italy's musicians.

CLAUDIO MONTEVERDI
Engraving published in Venice in 1644

13

MARC' ANTONIO CESTI'S 'IL POMO D'ORO'
Produced for the wedding of the Emperor Leopold I. Vienna, 1667
Engraving by Matthaeus Küsel after Lodovico Burnacini

II

'HIS BEST PUPIL WAS MOZART'

THERE is a temptation, not always resisted, to jump from Monteverdi to Alessandro Scarlatti as the next of the high peaks in the range of Italian opera, crediting him with the invention of the *da capo* aria and the foundation of the classical Italian *opera seria*. Much water however had flowed under many bridges between *L'Incoronazione di Poppea* and the first appearance of Scarlatti as an opera composer: in other words, several composers had contributed in the meantime towards a change. For instance there was Carissimi (1604–74) who, though not primarily an opera composer, played a leading part in the development of music in general and was probably the master of Scarlatti; there was Stradella, a shadowy, incredibly romantic figure (1642–85), always in fear of assassination and in fact finally assassinated as a penalty for his elopement with a young Venetian lady, but known to musicians nowadays primarily as the source from which Handel purloined material for *Israel in Egypt*.

Most important of all there was Cavalli (1602–76), the devoted disciple and friend of Monteverdi, who, perhaps more than any other man, may be credited or saddled with the responsibility for the definite break with the

14

original Florentine operatic tradition. Cavalli had a remarkable gift for melody. His music possessed a spontaneity which seemed quite new, and he showed a preference for musical form and expression for their own sake, as distinct from Monteverdi, whose music was always to some extent conditioned by the dramatic needs of a situation. He undoubtedly laid the foundation on which later arose what one of our more austere musicologists has called the "unfortunate aria form"; he wrote several highly successful operas and was responsible during his visits to France for introducing the music and ideals of Monteverdi to that country. In short, a man of uncommon parts.

Nevertheless it was Alessandro Scarlatti who summed up, and finally fixed, all that had preceded him in the evolution of music. Scarlatti has been called the founder of the famous Neapolitan school of opera but this is a little misleading. To begin with, he was not a Neapolitan but a Sicilian, born at Palermo in 1659. Moreover his first operas were written in Rome, not in Naples, where he went for the first time in 1684, remaining for eighteen years; after which he spent four years in Florence, Rome, Venice and Urbino successively. In 1708 he returned to Naples where, except for a three years' interval in Rome, he remained till his death in 1725. These changes of domicile are more important than is habitually realized because in those days Italy was in actual fact the "geographical expression" of later Victorian parlance; and the conditions at the various provincial capitals differed widely.

To the average modern reader Scarlatti remains a very shadowy figure sometimes confused with his equally famous son Domenico, now exclusively associated with the clavicembalo as virtuoso and composer alike. One of the reasons may be that he always remained a craftsman like so many Italian composers in those and subsequent days, expecting, and perhaps delighting, to fall in with the different material at his disposal and the different tastes of his audiences wherever he happened to be. Artistic craftsmen make little appeal to the imagination of the public, but Scarlatti's virtuosity is so amazing that, were it known, the public might for once revise their ideas. He wrote some 115 operas, some 600 cantatas, to say nothing of at least 15 oratorios and so much other music, both for ecclesiastical and secular purposes, that it can scarcely be enumerated.

Had even a considerable portion of this enormous output been mechanical and dull there might be little call for enthusiasm; but it was not. Here we are only concerned with the operas. Each of these as a rule contains some fifty arias, of which a large proportion represents some of the most beautiful melodies ever written. Very many of the scores of the operas are lost and it may be doubted whether even one of his serious operas is known in its entirety to present-day amateurs, however zealous. *Mitridate Eupatore*, written for Venice in 1707, *Tigrane* and his last opera *Griselda*, both written for Naples in 1715 and 1721 respectively, may tentatively be cited as the three best.

Scarlatti's operas are to the moderns as unapproachable as Monteverdi's and, when known, less palatable. Nevertheless Alessandro Scarlatti was one of the very great composers. In the words of his English biographer, Professor Dent, "before 1700, he had gathered up all that was best of the tangled materials produced by that age of transition and experiment, the seventeenth century, to form out of them a musical language, vigorous and flexible as Italian itself, which has been the foundation of all music of the classical period. Lesser composers contributed their part to this great work, but . . . the main glory of the achievement is certainly due to him. His best pupil, we may safely say, is Mozart."

This seems the right place to say something about the classical Italian *opera seria*, indissolubly linked with the name of Alessandro Scarlatti. Every aspect of it was highly conventionalized. In the music there was a rigid distinction between the recitative and the aria, which was of course of the *da capo* form familiarized in England by Handel. Scarlatti did not invent this form but he definitely established it. It has always been particularly disliked by musicologists who, not without reason, consider it incompatible with dynamic dramatic expression and movement. But the *opera seria*, almost deliberately it would seem, set out to eschew the dynamic in its arias, such dramatic movement as there was being confined to the recitative. Everything was essentially dignified, to the extent of definite pomposity. Up to the time of Scarlatti's death one exception could be found to this generality, in that there were comic characters in several of the operas, who even at times indulged in parodies of the behaviour and emotions of the main characters. Later however these ceased to exist and initiated a new operatic form of their own, leaving the *opera seria* to pursue, uncontaminated, its placid and dignified way without any relief whatever.

The texts were at least as conventionalized as the music itself, and more stilted, so that Kretzschmar could justly define Venetian opera in the latter half of the seventeenth century as being built on the formula "Two, four or six lovers matched with one, three or five princesses". Mythological began to be supplanted by historical personages, very important of course, and incredibly noble, who might operatically disagree but would never under any circumstances lose their tempers like ordinary human beings.

16

CAVALLI'S 'HIPERMESTRA' (1658)
Act III, sc. 2: Hipermestra throws herself from the tower

The presentation of operatic performances to the public also contributed to the eventual and definitive formation of *opera seria*. Very soon after the opening of the first public operatic theatre, similar theatres began rapidly to multiply. Even in Cavalli's time there were five of them in Venice alone, and they were soon to be found in varying numbers all over Italy. Now the taste of this new public enthusiastically and progressively favoured singers and singing; in other words what they wanted was primarily a number of arias. These the public theatres could supply, whereas their spectacular and instrumental resources perforce remained inferior to those at the performances of the early aristocratic opera. For some time operatic performances in the palaces of the great continued *pari passu* with public operatic performances. Moreover new orchestral possibilities were gradually discovered by composers, Alessandro Scarlatti especially; it was he who first established the horn as a normal orchestral instrument, and he must have the credit for fixing the form of the Italian *sinfonia* which served as an overture. Still, by the beginning of the eighteenth century what in *opera seria* remained univers-ally predominant were the aria and the singer of the aria.

The reader accustomed to modern conditions and to a modern point of view must find it difficult to understand how this *opera seria*, so static, so conventional in its form, swept Europe as it did and maintained its hegemony so long. It enjoyed undisputed primacy for more than half a century, and with some modifications retained public favour for many years after that. Apart from Italy itself it reigned, almost unchallenged, in Vienna where not only imported Italian composers but eventually Mozart wrote *opere serie* (*Idomeneo* and *La Clemenza di Tito*). It spread to Germany, and the con-summate Handel came originally to England as its protagonist and in fact wrote more operas than oratorios. His Italian competitors such as Bononcini and Porpora were equally in evidence. In France, despite the existence of a definite French operatic tradition, *opera seria* firmly established itself.

So unpalatable, so alien has the form become to us that few modern audiences could sit through a performance on the original lines, though some of Handel's operas (*Giulio Cesare*, *Rodelinda*, *Serse*) were successfully revived in Germany between the two wars. The lack of movement, the long-held gestures, the incessant posturings are tedious in the extreme. It is something of a tragedy because—as anybody at all familiar with Handel's *opere serie* will realize—they contain some of the most beautiful music ever written. But the form itself has effectually stifled them.

Few conversant with the facts will deny that the long vogue of the *opera seria* was mainly due to the popularity and the talents of the *castrati* who interpreted it. The whole subject of the *castrati* is somewhat delicate, and in England has been enveloped by musicologists in a kind of mist of reticence that leaves the reader more confused than before. Their oblique, half-casual references to male sopranos and male altos not improbably suggests to him those excellent gentlemen who sing falsetto in English Cathedral choirs; but the tone of the *castrati*, likened by Dr. Burney to that of a silver trumpet, bore no relation whatever to falsetto.

There is no necessity to discuss the physical aspect of the operation which enabled boys with exceptional voices to preserve them unbroken for the rest of their lives. The practice, very old, which was introduced into Italy either from Spain or from the Orient, was known in the twelfth century and common in the sixteenth when, owing to the difficulty of polyphonic music, *castrati* were preferred to boys in church choirs. They were associated with opera from its very beginning and the title-role of Monteverdi's *Orfeo* was sung by one of them. But with the opening of public theatres and the growing

SCENE FROM HANDEL'S 'GIULIO CESARE'
Anonymous caricature (formerly attributed to Hogarth)

demand for first-class singers consequent upon this the supply inevitably increased. In the first instance the employment of *castrati* was confined to male roles but in the latter years of the seventeenth century, owing to a certain prejudice against women on the stage and, in Rome, a positive Papal prohibition, they began to take female roles as well. Even Goethe, who started with a strong prejudice against *castrati* in women's roles, ended by preferring them on the interesting ground that their use emphasized the artificial conventionalism of the stage. The modern reader inclined to be shocked may usefully be reminded that the seventeenth century would have been equally surprised and even more shocked by the spectacle of a female Cherubino or Octavian—to say nothing of the "principal boy" in an English pantomime.

More important however is the fact that to their contemporaries the silver-trumpet-like tones of some of them represented nothing effeminate but the tonic attributes of perpetual youth, just as tenors today represent to us exuberance and dramatic intensity. Nor is this so surprising when we remember that many of the *castrati* lived normal and exceedingly active lives. Take

FARINELLI IN GALA DRESS
Pen drawing attributed to Antonio Maria Zanetti

the greatest of them, the soprano Farinelli; he lived to be seventy-seven and after his retirement from the stage became a political person of the first importance in Spain.

What matter to us here are their purely musical attributes. Even Voltaire, who disapproved of *castrati*, admitted that their voices were more beautiful than those of women, while Goethe talks of them as "beautiful and caressing". More important was the use they made of their voices. Never before and never since has the world known such singers. This is not surprising, for the attainment of perfection in the art of singing was a *castrato*'s whole life, and it was usual for him in old age to take pupils and thus hand on his experience. The technical accomplishments of a man such as Farinelli seem incredible nowadays. On one occasion, we are told, in rivalry with a famous trumpet player, he did a trill of a third, and then, when the trumpeter had given up for want of breath, made a *crescendo*, trilled again and finished with a perfect, very rapid and difficult *vocalise*. Doubtless Farinelli was the most gifted of them, but all could so to say compete. Complications of what now seem impossible *fioriture* they took in their stride.

Many people imagine that such acrobatics represent the sum total of their achievement; it was not so. Metastasio and other theorists condemned preoccupation with vocal fireworks as complete and obvious decadence. Moreover we know that contemporary audiences were not merely astonished by their singing, but deeply moved by it. Indeed this is the crux of the whole matter. The *castrati*, at least equally with the composers, provided the emotional and expressive element in *opera seria*. Many of them, it must be remembered, were admirable, highly trained musicians, so that when—as was expected in those days—they added their own embellishments to the composer's vocal line, these embellishments remained musically consonant. It is only when all this is fully realized that the long and otherwise inexplicable hegemony of the *opera seria* with its endless succession of *da capo* arias can be understood. The much berated repetitions were not mere repetitions; they were repetitions with a difference which, moreover, being often improvised, might vary from performance to performance. Not even the *castrati* could make *opera seria* dramatic but thanks to their wonderful voices, their consummate technique and their sensitive musicianship they could, and did, prevent their audience from finding it dull.

'ONE GOD, ONE FARINELLI'
Detail from Hogarth's 'The Rake's Progress', Plate 2

21

III

THE RISE OF THE PRIMADONNA

AFTER Alessandro Scarlatti's death in 1725 the reign of *opera seria* continued practically undisturbed for another thirty years. His mantle as a composer descended on the not unworthy shoulders of men such as Hasse, Jommelli and Traetta. All of them were highly gifted, all primarily concerned with melody. Jommelli also worked for the restoration of the importance of the orchestra and the greater freedom of writing for the different instruments; while Traetta in his middle and later years definitely broke new ground, notably in *Ifigenia*, written for Vienna, whereof the fine choruses certainly influenced Gluck. Hasse on the other hand remained consistently orthodox. In addition to much other music he wrote more than 100 operas, all singers' operas; he has indeed been described as the greatest composer of all time of purely singers' music. He was the personal friend and favourite of Metastasio—the arbiter of the then operatic elegances—all

22

of whose librettos he set to music, some of them two or three times over. Like Metastasio, he not only enjoyed the respect of all cultured amateurs but won and retained the affection of the general public. It was he whom the Neapolitans christened "il caro Sassone".

The other notable development during this period was the rise of the primadonna. Despite prejudice, despite Papal prohibitions it was not long before women achieved a position in the operatic theatre almost equal to that of the *castrati*. Female sopranos, if not altos, became as important as their male counterparts, while tenor parts were still as a rule reserved for villains, and basses (being regarded as comic) scarcely figured in *opera seria* at all.

Very soon after the middle of the eighteenth century ominous creaks and rumblings announced that all was not well with the structure of *opera seria*. Symptoms of revolt had appeared before then. For instance in 1720 an aristocratic, highly cultivated Venetian, Benedetto Marcello, an exceptionally

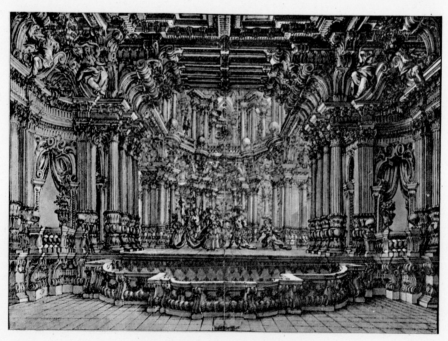

STAGE DESIGN FOR AN OPERA SERIA
By Giuseppe Galli da Bibiena (1696–1756)

gifted composer, attacked operatic conditions in a satirical pamphlet, *Il Teatro alla Moda*. This created a great stir, being frequently reprinted in subsequent years. It is a most diverting work, consisting of sarcastic advice to the composer, the librettist and, not least, the singers whose vanity and pretensions Marcello obviously found intolerable—an opinion that became increasingly rife as the century progressed.

Any definite attempt, however, to change the operatic form as such did not take place till the 1760's. Conventionally this is associated with the name of Gluck, but in fact the movement was to some extent general. If the credit for it should be assigned to any one individual it should be Calzabigi rather than Gluck.

The first conspiracy against *opera seria* seems to have been hatched in Vienna; which is not as odd as it may appear at first sight because in the matter of opera Vienna at that time was as Italian as any Italian city. There lived Metastasio as court-poet, the high priest of *opera seria* on the aesthetic and literary side, and it was against Metastasio that the movement was primarily directed. Those who dismiss Metastasio as of no account may usefully be reminded that Voltaire said that he was greater than the Greeks, equal to Corneille and Racine at their best. Needless to say, such praise is ludicrously exaggerated; the truth was stated by Metastasio himself when he jestingly suggested as an opening phrase of an autobiography that he never wrote: "In the middle of the eighteenth century there lived a certain

BENEDETTO MARCELLO
Contemporary engraving

PIETRO METASTASIO
Engraving by Paolo Caronni

CHRISTOPH WILLIBALD GLUCK
Painting attributed to Greuze

Abate Metastasio, a tolerable poet among a lot of bad ones." But if a merely tolerable, he was certainly a genuine poet and moreover a skilful dramatist. It is as a writer of opera texts, not of literary tragedies, that he should be regarded, for his verses, whether in aria or in recitative, were always written with a view to music. As such, despite our current prejudices, he must be reckoned a real master. Certainly not till Gluck met Calzabigi, possibly not till Verdi found Boito, was any opera composer to have such a gifted collaborator. For years his texts provided the standard librettos of *opera seria*, and many of them were set to music by dozens of different composers. His word made operatic law throughout Europe; at Vienna he was powerful at Court, popular in society and omnipotent in the theatre. Truly a formidable antagonist to challenge.

Nevertheless the challenge was launched; at first very tentatively, almost in secret. The original challenger was a certain Count Durazzo. This remarkable man, a Genoese of noble family, was appointed Intendant of the Vienna Opera in 1754. It seems clear that from the outset he disliked the smooth Metastasio, certainly as an author, possibly as a man; he was tired of the Metastasio formula of perpetual nobility, magnanimity and impeccability. He had to walk warily but was always on the lookout for instruments to further his design. The first of these instruments was the composer Gluck, for whom in 1755 he compiled, anonymously, a libretto, *L'Innocenza Giustificata*, which, though in the dedication it paid lip-service to Metastasio, was in fact the very antithesis of all that Metastasio stood for. It was not till the 'sixties, when the ballet-master Angiolini and the librettist Calzabigi arrived in Vienna, that Count Durazzo was able to bring his plans to fruition. Nevertheless it is remarkable that so little notice has been taken of him in the average musical history.

It may seem odd that Gluck, what we should now call a Czech, should figure so largely in an account of Italian Opera. But for the first fifty years of his life and more he, like Handel and Hasse, became by adoption an Italian opera composer. Even before he first came to Vienna in 1736 at the age of twenty-two he must have been subjected to Italian influences at the Jesuit college where he was educated as well as through Černohorsky, a Franciscan monk with previous musical experience at Padua and Assisi, who seems to have taught him composition. Gluck only stayed one year in Vienna; then Prince Melzi took him as his chamber musician to Milan, where he studied assiduously with Sammartini, till such time as, in Italy and elsewhere, he began the normal wandering life of the successful operatic composer. During these years he wrote nearly twenty operas, all in the current Italian convention, including several settings of librettos by Metastasio.

As a composer of such operas he seems to have been reckoned inferior, rather than superior, to his leading Italian contemporaries such as Jommelli and Traetta. Handel's famous remark, when he visited London with one of his early operas, to the effect that Gluck knew no more counterpoint than Handel's cook, was a just though of course exaggerated criticism of his clumsiness in handling pure music. But Gluck's forte was dramatic not pure music, and of this there are traces even in the early Italian operas.

It was not till he became associated, as Kapellmeister of the Vienna Opera, with Count Durazzo that his particular attributes were recognized as outstanding. Durazzo may well have welcomed Gluck almost as much for his defects as for his merits. He was not interested in contrapuntal skill and fluent writing so much as in passion, force and dramatic expression, in all of which the fiery, somewhat aggressive Gluck excelled. Even before he came to Vienna Gluck may well have had doubts about the universal validity of the Metastasian ideal because in Italy itself there were many signs of dissatisfac-

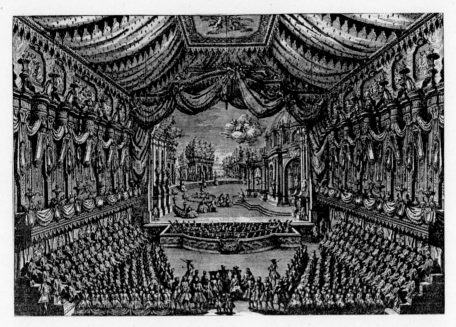

AN OPERA PERFORMANCE IN NAPLES, 1740
'Il Sogno d'Olimpia', text by Calzabigi, music by Giuseppe di Maio

tion and revolt. But in Vienna they began to crystallize. In addition to the Intendant himself there was Angiolini, the ballet-master, rival of the famous Noverre, but an equally convinced exponent of the theory that, in the dance, mime and dramatic action were more important than technical virtuosity or mere grace. Gluck seems soon to have made friends with him, for in 1761 they collaborated in a dramatic ballet, *Don Juan*, which was a complete antithesis to the merely decorative ballet current in Italy.

Most important of all, in 1761, there arrived in Vienna Ranieri Calzabigi, the man destined definitely to establish the new revolutionary principles. Half crook, half genius, and a friend of Casanova (whom he much resembled), Calzabigi proved exactly the man Durazzo and Gluck had been waiting for. If only from his Bohemian way of life, he was opposed to the punctiliousness of Metastasio, both in his private and professional capacity. Moreover he had been much influenced by French ideas. The year 1762 saw the beginning of his collaboration with Gluck: the opera *Orfeo*, whose novelty produced a great impression at the time and which still remains today the best-known of Gluck's operas. Certain concessions to the Metastasian ideal, notably the happy ending, may still be observed but it did mark the first appearance of undisguised revolt, further emphasized five years later in their opera *Alceste*, where there are no concessions whatever.

It is obvious therefore that the credit for the operatic "reform" conventionally associated with the name of Gluck alone should also be shared certainly by Calzabigi and probably by Durazzo as well. Moreover it was in origin essentially an Italian movement; which is the reason why some account of it should figure in a history of Italian opera. Calzabigi's primacy remains beyond question. Whether it be true or not, as he claimed, that he himself pointed out the actual musical stresses that Gluck should use in setting his libretto, he undoubtedly gave shape to the new operatic ideal alike as regards subject and text. The famous dedication of the score of *Alceste*, though signed by Gluck, was, in the words of Gluck's most learned and intelligent biographer, "of course written by Calzabigi". Finally there is the testimony of Gluck himself who, many years later, after the two collaborators had quarrelled, wrote in a French journal: "I should reproach myself even more grievously if I consented to let the invention of the new style of Italian opera be attributed to me. It is to M. Calzabigi that the principal merit belongs; and if my music has had some success, I think it my duty to recognize that I am beholden for it to him, since it was he who enabled me to develop the resources of my art."

Nevertheless it was Gluck's music that gave vitality and permanence to the new ideals. The exceptional sensitiveness and expressiveness of the accompanied recitative that now definitely superseded the old *recitativo secco* in serious opera, the dramatic power of his choruses and ballets, the poignancy of the music as a whole have kept it alive to this day. It may be doubted whether Gluck was ever what we today call an intellectual; like all his contemporaries he was primarily a craftsman, though a craftsman with a strong emotional bias, always ready to make use of the material and opportunities at his disposal. It is significant that even between *Orfeo* and *Alceste* he reverted on several occasions to conventional *opera seria*, including a libretto by the arch-enemy Metastasio himself. He wrote *Orfeo* for a *castrato*. In short, in Italy (which operatically included Vienna) he was a typical Italian composer. We are not concerned here with what he produced in France; when he went there, taking *Orfeo* and *Alceste* with him for adaptation to French taste, and wrote *Armide* and the two *Iphigénie*s he became to all intents and purposes a French composer, just as formerly he had been an Italian composer. Gluck was never, like Handel or Mozart, super-national.

HARLEQUIN
French woodcut, c. 1577

IV

ROUGH, RUDE AND INTENSELY LOCAL

THOUGH few people realize the fact it was the rise of *opera buffa* rather than the Gluck-Calzabigi "reforms" that mainly determined the ultimate supersession of *opera seria*. In reality these "reforms" represented only a swing of the pendulum, a manifestation of the perpetual tug-of-war between the claims of music and text which has always character-ized operatic activity and is by no means decided yet. The Gluck-Calzabigi movement might indifferently be described as "Back to Monteverdi" or "Forward to Wagner". *Opera buffa* on the other hand, in the course of its evolution, achieved something new and permanent; without it modern opera would scarcely have come into being.

Before sketching the purely musical development of *opera buffa* the nature of the soil in which it took root should be indicated. *Opera buffa* was the direct descendant, if not the actual product, of the *commedia dell' arte* whereof the origin goes far back in the history of European civilization, certainly to the Romans. The *commedia dell' arte* had nothing to do with art; probably the best English equivalent is "the artisans' comedy", and possibly the title itself was coined by the fashionables as a term of derision. The *commedia dell' arte* was quintessentially popular, rough, rude and intensely local. The dialogue was always improvised and the actors wore masks. The characters were immutably fixed by tradition and associated with the various Italian cities, Venice and Naples in particular. Thus Pantaleone, our modern Pantaloon, was an elderly Venetian; Arlecchino (Harlequin) and Brighella came from Bergamo; the pedantic, rather ridiculous Dottore from Bologna. Pulcinella, the protagonist of Punch and Judy, and Scaramuccia, the fiery, boastful military adventurer, were both Neapolitan. There were many minor masks from other Italian cities such as Stenterello in Florence, Beltrame in Milan, and so on, but those from Venice, Bergamo and Naples had undisputed precedence, and, though each spoke in his native dialect, became national figures.

When later Goldoni, the famous Venetian dramatist, began to write his comedies, abolishing the masks and providing the characters with written instead of improvised dialogue, no fundamental change in the structure or the quality of the entertainment took place, at any rate at first. It remained funny rather than witty, boisterous, full of exuberant vitality and high spirits, with a rapidity of movement and a series of conventions typical and unaltered. What Metastasio had been to *opera seria*, Goldoni almost, if not quite, was to *opera buffa*.

Even in the seventeenth century comic characters had been introduced into *opera seria*, though remaining outside the principal framework; and Alessandro Scarlatti himself wrote two full-dress comic operas of which one, *Il Trionfo dell' Onore*, has recently been revived. For our purpose however *opera buffa* may be regarded as having first begun in the form of *intermezzi*. These *intermezzi* were given between the acts of an *opera seria* and consisted as a rule of two or three characters only, these being the direct or indirect descendants of the old masks. The most famous of them all is Pergolesi's *La Serva Padrona*, originally produced in 1733 between the acts of an *opera seria* of his own.

In recent years there has been a tendency to write down Pergolesi among musicologists, who quote with approval old Paisiello's malicious dictum to the effect that, had Pergolesi lived longer, his reputation would have waned rather than waxed. Before however congratulating Pergolesi on his premature demise at the age of twenty-six, it is well to remind ourselves that *La Serva Padrona* has at all times commanded the enthusiastic affection of musicians, not least Beethoven. In Pergolesi's own day his *opere serie*, of which the best, *L'Olimpiade*, produced the year before he died, is character-

GIOVANNI BATTISTA PERGOLESI
Engraving by Wintier

ized by just those qualities of sweetness and naturalness that still keep his *Stabat Mater* in our musical repertory, were at least equally esteemed. His contemporaries, not to mention himself, would have been surprised and probably shocked had they known that he would be remembered first and foremost by a mere *intermezzo*. Still, this is what has happened, and not without reason. *La Serva Padrona* remains a little masterpiece of bustle, intrigue and humorous characterization. The Italians took it to their heart at once, and when, in the middle of the century, it was introduced into France it took the country by storm. Rameau said that, had he been thirty years younger, he would have gone to school again with the composer; while Rousseau and the Encyclopaedists lauded the little opera to the skies as usefully consonant with their theories.

In a very short time *opera buffa* ceased to be confined to *intermezzi*. A year or two before the production of *La Serva Padrona*, Leo (1694–1744) had begun writing genuine comic operas at Naples, where he was later followed by Logroscino (1700–63), whose productions were so successful that the Neapolitans christened him "the God of Comic Opera", and who has been credited with the invention of the concerted finale. As evidence of the strong tie that still bound *opera buffa* to the traditions of the masks it is worth noting that both these composers wrote not in standard Italian but in the Neapolitan

31

dialect. The same phenomenon may be observed in Venice, where Galuppi in his comic operas enjoyed the advantage of being able to collaborate with Goldoni himself; and he of course used Venetian.

But whatever the language, the characteristics, both of music and of text, remained much the same. The music with its rapid *recitativo secco* sparkled and bubbled like a fast-flowing stream, occasionally pausing for an arietta or a duet. The characters remained variations more or less of the original *commedia dell' arte* models, though they had now acquired names and personalities of their own. The pedantic, silly and jealous old father or guardian, the intriguing servant, the swashbuckling adventurer, the thwarted lovers—even today we recognize them all. There were no *castrati* of course; the bass singer, banished from *opera seria*, entered into full possession of his rightful domain, which then included a capacity to sing the most difficult and florid music; the tenor, instead of being a villain, began to be identified with the attributes of virtue and heroism which he has never since lost. They laughed, they even cried, they quarrelled among themselves like ordinary human beings. It was the humanity and the naturalness of *opera buffa* that were to ensure its triumph.

During the eighteenth century three composers stand out as exponents of what henceforward it is more correct to call comic opera than *opera buffa*: Piccini, Paisiello and Cimarosa. The modern reader knows the first of these mainly if not exclusively by the celebrated Gluck-Piccini feud that raged in Paris in the 1780's. Far too much importance has been given to this; it was in fact what we should nowadays call a mere journalistic or society squabble. Neither Gluck nor Piccini approved of it, and Piccini in particular, a most simple and generous man, was at considerable pains to avoid taking part in it. On Gluck's death it was Piccini who launched a campaign to perpetuate his memory by an annual concert. Padre Martini, the celebrated pedagogue, when asked to take sides in the dispute, summed up its absurdity once and for all: "Since the characteristic style of the one", he wrote, "was quite different from that of the other I had every reason to praise them both without blaming or prejudging either."

This purely Parisian episode scarcely falls within the scope of this book but its absurdity must be stressed in justice to Piccini, who seems too often to be deemed a mere presumptuous weakling as compared with the mighty Gluck. He was nothing of the kind; he was a very good composer, whose forte however lay less in a tragic than a humorous and especially a sentimental vein, though his tragic opera *Didone* has been highly praised by musicologists. Piccini was born at Bari in 1728 and he first achieved outstanding success

DOMENICO CIMAROSA
Contemporary painting

with the opera *La Buona Figliuola*, otherwise known as *Cecchina*, produced in
Rome in 1760. With a libretto by Goldoni (a free adaptation of Richardson's
novel *Pamela*), *Cecchina* caused a furore similar to that which more elderly
readers may remember as associated with the appearance of Du Maurier's
Trilby. It has been said that as comic operas pure and simple later works of
his, such as *Le Faux Lord* and *La Molinarella*, both produced in Paris after
Didone, are superior but there can be no doubt that as an entity *Cecchina*
stands on a pedestal apart. The gayer portions already foreshadowed Cimarosa, the character-drawing was fresh and the sentimental charm of the
music quite irresistible. Verdi, when asked by Boito to make a list of the
half-dozen old Italian composers who should be studied with a view to
choral compositions, included Piccini among them, claiming (rightly or
wrongly) that he was the first to write quintets and sextets, and that
Cecchina should be considered the first genuine comic opera. Piccini, unlike

Gluck, had the misfortune to live through the Revolution and died in poverty at Passy in 1800.

Paisiello was born at Taranto in 1740. A greater contrast to the kindly, sweet-tempered, unassertive Piccini can scarcely be imagined. Paisiello was malicious, spiteful and a born intriguer, though no one would guess this from his music, of which the outstanding characteristics are tenderness and genuine, if limited, pathos rather than humour. His output, like that of most of his contemporaries, was enormous. In addition to much other music of all kinds he wrote more than a hundred operas and, again like his other successful contemporaries, he spent much of his time abroad in various European capitals, though he began and ended his musical career at Naples where in 1816 he died, politically disgraced owing to his miscalculated efforts always to be on the winning side. As regards comedy his comic operas were not remarkably successful. One however, *Il Socrate Immaginario*, written early in his career, sounds very promising. While attached to the Court at St. Petersburg he tried characteristically, but unsuccessfully, to score off Pergolesi by re-setting *La Serva Padrona*; and it was there too that he first set *The Barber of Seville* to music with, as it seemed at the time, complete success. Not till more than thirty years later did Rossini, by means of the greatly superior *Barber* that we all know, hoist the old man with his own petard. Not that Paisiello's *Barber*, extremely popular for many years, was worthless. It has even been claimed that the sentimental passages are superior to Rossini's.

Possibly Paisiello's best operas were *La Bella Molinara* and *Nina, o la Pazza per Amore*, written in 1788 and 1789. The light sentimental pathos of the former is said to have moved audiences to tears, an unprecedented event. Hence comes too the air by which Paisiello is best remembered today, "Nel cor più non mi sento", which had the honour of serving as a theme for a set of variations by Beethoven. *Nina* was even more successful, perhaps because the synthetic pastoral atmosphere so felicitously translated by Paisiello into music provided just the escape from the ugly troublous times that everybody was longing for. We know that it especially appealed to Napoleon. Indeed in the early 1800's Paisiello became his favourite composer and was commissioned to write the music for his coronation.

The comic operas of both Piccini and Paisiello differed considerably from the old *opera buffa*. Sentiment, almost unknown in *opera buffa*, played a large part in them; they were unquestionably influenced by the French *genre larmoyant*. This however is not true of the most important of the three, Domenico Cimarosa. Born at Aversa near Naples in 1749, Cimarosa achieved his first outstanding success in his early twenties with the opera *Le Stravaganze del Conte* and, except in *opera seria* for which he had little aptitude, remained more or less consistently successful till his death in 1801 at Venice whither, after a term of imprisonment and the return of the Bourbons to Naples, he had been exiled for having written a *Carmagnola Napoletana*. Like Paisiello he was incredibly prolific—his operas number nearly 80 and his chamber music some 500 pieces—and like both Paisiello and Piccini he spent much of his life in foreign capitals. There however the resemblance ends. Fat, jolly, enjoying life to the full and as modest and kindly as Paisiello was the reverse, Cimarosa indulged very little in sentiment; he was first and foremost a real *opera buffa* man, a direct descendant of the composer of *La Serva Padrona* whose style he enlarged and brought to perfection.

He is best known to us through his still popular *Il Matrimonio Segreto*, but other full-dress comic operas such as *Le Astuzie Femminili* (revived by Diaghileff in London some thirty years ago) and *Giannina e Bernardone* were highly successful in their day not only in Italy but abroad. Still, *Il Matrimonio Segreto* remains his masterpiece, indeed one of the three or four great masterpieces of Italian comic opera. There never was gayer music, more sparkle and rapidity of movement, slyer humour and characterization than in this enchanting comedy of domestic intrigue. Even the more or less sentimental music for the two lovers, who had by now definitely established their claims to equality of importance in comic opera, is frivolous without ceasing to be tender. Cimarosa wrote *Il Matrimonio Segreto* in Vienna in 1792, where it so pleased the Emperor that he ordered its repetition from beginning to end after supper had been served to everybody concerned—surely the most flattering encore in the annals of music.

The historical importance of *Il Matrimonio Segreto* can scarcely be over-stressed in that it remains the link between the original *opera buffa* and the eighteenth-century comic opera deriving from it, to culminate, through the subsequent masterpieces of Rossini and Donizetti, in Verdi's *Falstaff*. Produced as it was a year after the death of Mozart, it must be excluded from the Italian influences that played so large a part in the fashioning of the greatest of all operatic masters; for without Paisiello, Piccini, Pergolesi and the Italian *opera buffa* composers in general the supreme masterpieces *Così Fan Tutte*, *Le Nozze di Figaro* and *Don Giovanni* could scarcely have come to birth. Yet some of the earlier operas of Cimarosa, very popular in Germany, may well have contributed their quota in forming Mozart's appreciation of the value of rapid movement. Cimarosa at least, who once described Mozart as the equivalent in music of Raphael, would have been pleased to think so.

V

A CYNIC AMUSED

THREE composers of eminence survived Gluck to carry on the theories of operatic "reform" associated with his name: Salieri, Cherubini and Spontini.

Little need be said about Salieri (1758–1825), known nowadays solely on account of his disagreement with Mozart and the legend, totally unfounded, that he poisoned him. In recalling Mozart's dislike of Salieri we must remember that he had no high opinion of Gluck either; and Salieri, though a composer of parts, was certainly not Gluck's equal. Yet Beethoven thought highly of him and, when setting Italian words to music, frequently sought his advice. He wrote operas in French and German as well as in Italian, of which at least two, *La Grotta di Trofonio* and *Axur*, both produced in Vienna where he was Master of the Music, enjoyed outstanding success in his lifetime.

Cherubini (1768–1842) was a composer on an altogether higher plane. To have been described by Beethoven as, after Beethoven himself, the best composer in Europe and the greatest dramatic composer of the age is an appraisement that cannot lightly be dismissed, the more so because Beethoven, when writing *Fidelio*, translated his admiration into the sincerest form of flattery. Yet Cherubini must play a minor role in this book. His operas, even *Les Deux Journées*, are scarcely known to present-day audiences except by their overtures, whereas his fine church music remains comparatively familiar. Moreover, though he began his career in Italy and in fact wrote many Italian operas, mostly in a light vein, all his best work was produced in Paris, where he spent the last fifty-four years of his life, becoming in fact Director of the Conservatoire. From the beginning of the nineteenth century onwards it becomes increasingly difficult to decide which of the many Italian composers who worked or settled in Paris should be regarded as the exponents of the Italian or the French operatic school. In Cherubini's case however there is little doubt; he became definitely gallicized, and neither *Médée* nor *Les Deux Journées* nor *Anacréon* can be considered as Italian operas, though *Les Deux Journées*, with its new and beautiful treatment of ensemble, had considerable influence in Italy.

Spontini (1774–1851), though scarcely equal to Cherubini as a musician, is more important for our present purposes. Like Cherubini, he started his career by writing in Italy many operas of the lighter kind and spent most of his life abroad—in Berlin, and in Paris where his three main operas, *La Vestale*, *Fernand Cortez* and *Olympie*, were produced. Of Gluck's three successors he was the most like his master in that he specialized in highly dramatic orchestral contrasts, and his music in general showed much vigour and nobility. Indeed nobility, sometimes a little stilted it is true, was Spontini's forte, the outstanding impression made on us even today by *La Vestale* and *Olympie*, both of which have been successfully revived in recent years. In private life he was conceited and decidedly pompous. Nothing could be more revealing than the self-portrait depicted in the quite astonishing statement he made in the course of an argument with Wagner six years before he died: "How can anybody write anything new seeing that I, Spontini, declare that I cannot do better than I have done! Besides I know that since *La Vestale* not a note has been written which has not been stolen from my music."

Despite this bombast his real genius is undoubted, for his operas exercised great influence everywhere. He commanded the respect and the admiration of all his most distinguished contemporaries, Wagner included. Incidentally he was the first of the modern virtuoso conductors, insisting on rigid discipline and striking effects of orchestral light and shade.

The main activities of these three men took place outside Italy. In Italy itself therefore the stage was clear for the appearance of that brilliant genius, Gioacchino Rossini, who, though he was born later than any of them, was

LUIGI CHERUBINI
Drawing by Horace Vernet

for practical purposes their contemporary and in fact ceased altogether to write operas many years before Cherubini and Spontini died. In any appraisement of Rossini this early cessation of his active life as a composer must never be forgotten, though it often is. He lived to be seventy-six but after the age of thirty-seven he never wrote an opera. He remains therefore a composer considerably more remote in time than the actual date of his death (1868) would suggest.

Rossini was no disciple of Gluck; with him the operatic pendulum swung back to the supremacy of music over text, though nobody knew better than he how to make capital out of a dramatic situation, tragic or comic. Born at Pesaro in 1792, the son of the town-crier, he seems to have had more difficulty than the average Italian composer in getting a start. It is usually said that he was too lazy or too naughty to complete his academic studies at Bologna. He was always inclined to be lazy and as a boy he was very naughty; but in this instance he was merely too poor, being forced at a very early age to make money to contribute to the family resources. At the age of eighteen he contrived to get a commission to write a one-act farcical opera for a theatre at Venice and during the next two or three years he specialized in little works of this kind and had considerable success with them. Even in

GASPARO SPONTINI
Drawing by Horace Vernet

those early days his music, irresponsible, impertinent and irresistibly gay, was recognized as having an unmistakable flavour of its own. Of these little comic operas none has achieved a place in the modern repertory; to us they are represented only by the delicious overture to *La Scala di Seta*, frequently performed by Beecham and Toscanini.

It was not till 1813 that Rossini wrote the opera destined to place him unquestionably ahead of his elder contemporaries such as Ferdinando Paer and the learned italianized German, Johann Mayr, from whom incidentally Rossini is said to have stolen the idea of his famous crescendo. Mayr was highly and rightly esteemed as an opera composer, but neither he nor Paer could compete with the freshness and the lyrical spontaneity of this young man of twenty-one. Certainly neither of them could have written "Di tanti palpiti", that aria from *Tancredi* which was so popular in Venice that every-one from gondoliers to members of the aristocracy sang snatches of it from morning till night. Still less perhaps could either of them have produced an *opera buffa* so completely successful, so gay and so original as *L'Italiana in Algeri*, with which Rossini delighted the Venetians only some three months after the production of *Tancredi*. Fortunately not only Italy but France and England have had the opportunity in recent years of judging the merits of this delightful work for themselves. Yet few people realize that it was written by a mere lad.

During the next two years he wrote another six operas of which only two need be mentioned, *Aureliano* because the overture was afterwards lifted and attached to *The Barber of Seville*, and *Elisabetta, Regina d'Inghilterra*. For several reasons *Elisabetta* is an important landmark in Rossini's career; it was the first of his operas to be performed under the management of the Neapolitan impresario Barbaia; it was written for, and inspired by, the Spanish prima-donna Isabella Colbran, whom he subsequently married; in it he first established the innovation of writing down exactly what the singers had to sing instead of conceding the latitude of embellishment and improvisation which they had for so long enjoyed. Rossini is said to have come to this decision after hearing the male soprano Velluti in *Aureliano*—almost the last appearance of a *castrato* in opera. Not apparently that he was so much dissatisfied with Velluti's performance as frightened by what might be the result had his music been left to the mercies of a singer with inferior musical training, one of the new now all-powerful tribe of primadonnas for instance. His friendship with Colbran and Barbaia at Naples enabled him to put this daring innovation into actual practice.

It was while on leave from Naples that Rossini wrote and produced for Rome the immortal *Barber of Seville*. The first performance on 20th February 1816 was a complete fiasco. Rossini, outwardly so flippant, so devil-may-care, but inwardly abnormally sensitive and nervous, retired to bed and ostensibly to sleep. At the second performance however it was clear that the fiasco had deliberately been manufactured owing to public dislike of the management. Paisiello and his still numerous adherents may have had something to do with it also, because Paisiello had already set the *Barber* to music and we know how vindictive and jealous he was. Still it must be remembered that nowhere was the *Barber* at first recognized as a masterpiece, though due recognition was not long in coming. Beethoven, Berlioz, Wagner and Brahms have all expressed their love for it, and with the public it remains no less a favourite than it was a hundred years ago.

Rossini wrote the music in a fortnight, perhaps thirteen days, as he told Wagner. Even if the incredible fluency of composers at that time be taken into account this seems miraculous; it is difficult to understand how in so short a time the notes could have been written down, much less thought of. Moreover, apart from the overture, he made very little use of music from previous operas as had been and was frequently to be his practice. The *Barber* is too familiar to need discussion but one feature of it may usefully

ROSSINI'S 'BARBER OF SEVILLE'
Lithograph from 'The Musical Bouquet', c. 1845

be pointed out: it is an ideal translation into music of Beaumarchais's play, better in this respect than Mozart's *Le Nozze di Figaro*, with much music too genuinely emotional. Rossini's music, like Beaumarchais's text, knows neither passion nor love; it is gallant, ironical, witty. In the opera as in the play the naughty Rosina, the dashing Count, the repulsive Bartolo, the unspeakable Basilio, all really move and have their being in the intrigues of Figaro. Which is just as it should be.

During the seven remaining years of Rossini's Italian career he was to produce seventeen operas, but of these only seven require specific mention. First *Otello*, produced in Naples at the end of the same year as witnessed the birth of the *Barber*. Of all Rossini's serious operas this is one of the best, the last act in particular being full of enchanting music. Indeed this always remained a special favourite of Rossini's, who bracketed it with the second act of *William Tell* and the whole of the *Barber* as the music by which he was most likely to be remembered. But for the modern public, especially an English public, the opera is hopelessly handicapped by the mishandling of Shakespeare—not to mention its inevitable supersession seventy years later by what is perhaps the greatest masterpiece of all Italian dramatic literature, Verdi's *Otello*.

Lablache   Dandini

1831

ROSSINI'S 'LA CENERENTOLA'
Luigi Lablache as Dandini
Water-colour by A. E. Chalon, 1831

The following year, 1817, witnessed the appearance of another two operas of outstanding merit: *La Cenerentola*, a highly mundane version of the Cinderella story, and an effective melodrama called *La Gazza Ladra* (The Thieving Magpie) to which is attached one of the best overtures that Rossini ever wrote; its opening drum-roll was considered so revolutionary that a conservative-minded student at Milan thought it his duty to threaten the composer with assassination. As for *La Cenerentola*, some think it as good as the *Barber*, but for various reasons it has never attained equal fame, primarily because it is notably more difficult to sing but also because the libretto is a trifle confused. Nevertheless Rossini's inspiration never shone more brightly than in the humorous sextet of the second act and the brilliant finale with the primadonna's famous run down from a top A to a low G sharp. Of all the Rossini revivals in recent years *La Cenerentola* has enjoyed, as it deserved, the greatest success.

There remain only *La Donna del Lago* (1819), a (for Rossini) strangely romantic opera based on Walter Scott, *Mosè* (1818), *Maometto II* (1820) and *Semiramide* (1823). Both *Mosè* and *Maometto* are only known to us in the revised versions made several years later in Paris, which do not therefore lie within the scope of this book. Still, the new paramount importance of the bass singer and the magnificent choral writing of *Mosè*, the beautiful music of the last act and the effective overture of *Maometto II*—at any rate when it became *La Siège de Corinthe*—cannot be overlooked.

The most important fact about *Semiramide* is the accident of its being the last opera written by Rossini for the Italian stage. Henceforward till the very end of his life he was to be domiciled in Paris. Unlike Cherubini however he never became truly gallicized. Indeed only two of his productions, the comic opera *Le Comte Ory* (1828) and *William Tell*, can be considered typically French. How and why Rossini ceased altogether writing operas after what is generally considered his greatest masterpiece I have discussed at length in my biography of the master. Suffice it to say here that it was primarily due to what would now be called a nervous breakdown, which effectively precluded his return to professional activity.

To return however for a moment to *Semiramide*; it was long considered the climax of Rossini's achievement in *opera seria* and in Italy preferred to

ROSSINI'S 'LA GAZZA LADRA'
Stage design for the Scala, Milan, 1817
Coloured engraving by Alessandro Sanquirico

43

William Tell. It has recently been revived and not without success because it does contain some very effective music, but it is too long and the convention remains very alien to us. The magnificent overture, however, still retains its hold on public affection. When Rossini wrote *Semiramide* he had never, except for a brief visit to Vienna the year previously, left Italy. Yet his reputation was now world-wide. In this very year 1823, we are told, at least twenty-three of his operas were being performed in various countries. Stendhal wrote of Rossini at this time: "The glory of this man is only limited by the limits of civilization itself; and he is not yet thirty-two."

This seems the right place to consider for one moment what operatic conditions in Italy were like when Rossini achieved his triumphs both at home and abroad. Little need be said about the comic operas: they were produced and performed in very much the same manner as today—except that they were less well played and far better sung. But the matter is quite different as regards the serious operas. Several things had changed since the palmy days of *opera seria*. The *da capo* aria for instance had disappeared and the *castrati* had practically ceased to exist. Nevertheless much of the old tradition persisted; a happy ending remained almost obligatory—Rossini's librettist in *Otello* provided one of incredible fatuity which almost suggests Desdemona and Othello ending the play with an appropriate song and dance—and the singers, male and female, were as capricious and as exacting as ever. Woe betide any composer who wrote a bar more for one primadonna than for another; the ladies counted them, just as modern film stars are said to measure the size of their illuminated names on Broadway. One of them, we are told, invariably insisted on her first aria containing the words "Felice ognora" because she found them particularly convenient for the display of her vocal technique. A certain Marchesi made a practice of refusing to sing unless his first entrance was made either on horseback or on the top of a hill, a helmet with white feathers not less than six feet high being indispensable in both instances. And since the singers were the public's primary concern, the unfortunate composer had little opportunity to make any effective protest.

The actual performances too would strike us nowadays as very odd. They were very long, lasting from about half past seven till after midnight, often with a ballet between the acts. Except at first nights nobody expected or was expected to listen to an opera in its entirety. During a mere recitative spectators paid calls on each other in the boxes or went out to patronize the gambling rooms, at that time a feature of every Italian opera house, while during the arias allotted to the secondary characters refreshments were served, so that these came to be known as *arie del sorbetto*. Needless to say

everybody talked at will—and it cannot honestly be said that this habit has
ceased in Italy even today. The explanation of all this lies in the fact that
opera was the only form of amusement available to Italians at that time;
there were no games, no theatres. The opera was synonymous with social life.

Rossini had neither the temperament nor the will-power to effect any
radical change in these matters. Despite the protests of some of his admirers
he did succeed in getting greater consideration for the orchestra, and his
overtures in particular achieved an importance hitherto unknown. He placed
a certain curb on the licence of his singers; but on the whole he remained
what he fundamentally was: a cynic amused rather than disgusted by all
these extravagances, tolerant, brilliant, facile. He was a great genius but
scarcely a great man; had he been he might well have attained to a position
among the greatest, instead of only among the most agreeable, composers.

'JOHN BULL AT THE ITALIAN OPERA'
Water-colour by Thomas Rowlandson, 1803

DONIZETTI'S 'L'ELISIR D'AMORE'
Luigi Lablache as Dr. Dulcamara
Coloured lithograph by J. Brandard, c. 1850

VI

THE LAST FRUIT OF OPERA BUFFA

ALTHOUGH Bellini and Donizetti both died before Rossini, most of their more important operas were produced after his retirement from active composition. They therefore serve as a bridge between him and the latter half of the nineteenth century. Instinctively we bracket them, but in truth no two composers could be more diverse.

Vincenzo Bellini, who was born at Catania, Sicily, in 1801, is one of the most romantic figures in the history of music. His early death at the age of thirty-four, his always fragile health and delicate appearance, the influence of at least three love affairs on his artistic production, make of him just the figure favoured by female novelists in search of a composer. Though by no means possessed of the fluency typical of so many of his Italian colleagues he produced in his short life eleven operas—the first, immediately successful, at the age of twenty-four while still a student at the Naples Conservatoire. Of these only four demand specific attention. *Il Pirata*, produced in Naples

'AN OVATION'
The singer is probably Giuditta Pasta in Donizetti's 'Anna Bolena'
Brown monochrome drawing, heightened with white, by A. E. Chalon

47

in 1827, two years after his first opera, is important not only because it already shows clearly Bellini's distinctive attributes as a composer but because, thanks largely to the magnificent singing of the tenor Rubini, it laid the foundation of his national and international fame. The year 1831 witnessed, at La Scala, Milan, the production of the two operas generally considered to be his masterpieces: *La Sonnambula* and *Norma*.

La Sonnambula, idyllic and sentimental, is of special interest to us in that it achieved its outstanding success in London, probably because Malibran sang it there in English. Unlike *Norma* however it seems to have passed definitely out of the modern repertory. Since in my view *Norma* is a work of the highest genius, this diversity of fortune does not seem to me unjustified. Even today, if singers of sufficient competence can be found, the music of *Norma* sounds as moving and as effective as ever. Yet the first night was so disastrous that the opera nearly perished at birth. Now we know that this was due not to the music but to the performance. Both *La Sonnambula* and *Norma* had been written for Giuditta Pasta, almost the only one of his primadonnas with whom Bellini does not seem to have been in love—but her husband apparently thought otherwise: for on the first night he indulged in such a scene of jealousy that the poor woman, not to mention the rest of the company, could hardly sing.

I Puritani, produced in Paris in 1835, owed a great deal to the friendly help and advice of Rossini, who urged on Bellini the claims of a rather more elaborate orchestration and a greater attention to the demands of the various dramatic situations. Since the composer died later in the same year we shall never know whether this opera might not have marked the beginning of a new stage in his career.

To faulty schooling has often been ascribed Bellini's contrapuntal weakness and poverty of orchestration. Without reason, however. From his very earliest years Bellini loved simplicity for its own sake, deliberately eschewing polyphony on the one hand and the vocal elaboration of Rossini on the other. What he loved was pure melody, and from *Il Pirata* to *I Puritani* it was in pure melody that he excelled. Nobody in the history of music has ever been able to achieve vocal phrases of such heavenly length. From this it follows that perfection of vocal interpretation is indispensable to his music—which is why nowadays we so rarely hear it performed. But in his lifetime Bellini was most fortunate in his interpreters. This was the last age of great singing. We have already taken note of his debt to the tenor Rubini; his debt to his primadonnas, Grisi, Pasta and Malibran, was at least as great. The fact that two of the three seem to have been in love with him may have

MARIA FELICITA MALIBRAN
Lithographed song cover, c. 1832

counted for something, especially since one of them was Malibran. This exceptional woman, born a Garcia, was almost as remarkable in her way as Farinelli himself. She had a magnificent voice and a perfect command of it; she wrote music; she was a painter of parts and a notable horsewoman. She died at the early age of twenty-eight, only a year after Bellini, of whose music she had become the acknowledged reigning interpreter throughout Europe.

Still, the greatness of Bellini's debt to his singers should not be allowed to obscure the real originality of his music. The elegiac beauty and dignity of *Norma* place that opera in a category of its own. Even Wagner recognized this; Verdi also. Much might be written too of the mutual reactions of Chopin and Bellini. The two men, so alike in appearance, character and destiny, became the most devoted of friends till death. The genesis of much of Chopin's melody must be sought in the Bellini arias he loved so well. Of all the secondary figures in the history of Italian opera Bellini remains perhaps the greatest, certainly the most individual.

There was a very real friendship also between Bellini and Donizetti at the height of their careers, but underneath this and their mutual admiration there lurked a curious substratum of jealousy. Bellini seems to have been afraid of Donizetti's superior technique while Donizetti, however reluctantly, always admitted the superiority of Bellini's melodic genius. Bellini is said to have been depressed by the excellence of Donizetti's *Anna Bolena* but Donizetti, more magnanimous, said in 1832, after the initial fiasco of *Norma*, that he would be proud to have written it.

The two men were fundamentally different in that among all the facile and fluent Italian composers of the age Donizetti was certainly the most facile and the most fluent. For instance he wrote a whole opera, *Maria di Rohan*, in eight days; about the same time was needed for *Lucrezia Borgia*, while the last (and best) act of *La Favorita* took him only a few hours. *Don Pasquale* was written in eleven days and scored in eight, the delicious servants' chorus in the last act having been turned out for the album of a friend in twenty-two minutes. So possibly the story is true that Donizetti, on being told that Rossini had taken only a fortnight to compose *The Barber of Seville*, exclaimed: "The lazy fellow!"

Donizetti, born in Bergamo in 1824, became a pupil of the gifted and competent Mayr, for whom he retained throughout his life a touching affection and an admiration so great that he once wrote: "Provided Mayr loves me nothing else would ever make me conceited". Almost his last act before he became insane was to pay a visit to the old man "because he is so old". Largely owing to Mayr's tuition he acquired a technique superior to that of most of his Italian colleagues. Unusually too he initiated his career by writing a number of string quartets, somewhat in the manner of Haydn, which are by no means devoid of interest. When some of them were revived in London a few years before the war they made quite a favourable impression.

Despite his facility Donizetti did not write an opera till he was twenty-one and achieved no real success till four years later when *Zoraide* was produced in Rome. He soon however made up for this tardiness by writing during the rest of his life, for Vienna and Paris as well as Italy, more than sixty other operas, of which only the outstanding can be mentioned here. In 1830 there was *Anna Bolena*, usually considered the first of his important works, after which old Mayr, it is said, consented for the first time to call him Maestro. In 1832 came the still popular *Elisir d'Amore* which, in addition to the justly beloved "Una furtiva lagrima", contains some delightfully fresh and spontaneous music. The three following years saw the production of a great quantity of operas, good, bad and indifferent, *Parisina* and *Lucrezia Borgia*

DONIZETTI'S 'LUCREZIA BORGIA'
Grisi and Mario as Lucrezia and Gennaro
Coloured lithograph by M. and N. Hanhart after J. Brandard, c. 1850

among them, culminating in 1835 with *Lucia di Lammermoor*, the best of all Donizetti's serious operas. It was soon after *Lucia* and the deaths of his wife, his mother and his father that the symptoms of the nervous depression, destined eventually to destroy his reason, were first noticeable. Even during the composition of *Lucia* he had complained of terrible headaches but in 1837 he was completely prostrated, so depressed indeed that he is said to have deliberately eaten every kind of food in the hope that he might catch the cholera then raging in Naples, and die.

51

By 1838 however he had sufficiently recovered to go to Paris to occupy there the place vacated by Rossini. His facility, momentarily lost, returned and, apart from refashioning completely the opera *Poliuto*, he wrote *The Daughter of the Regiment* and *La Favorita*, one of his better serious operas. In general his Paris operas may be considered superior to their predecessors; Wagner himself condescended to comment favourably on the greater care and the comparative lack of conventionalism shown in their composition. But like so many Italian composers in Paris, Donizetti seems to have suffered from homesickness and he actually took a few months' holiday in Italy and Switzerland (that is to say he wrote only one comic opera!) before being appointed to Vienna, where, despite the progressive return of his terrible headaches, he composed *Linda di Chamounix* and *Maria di Rohan*. He fortunately resisted disease long enough to write in 1843 for the Théâtre des Italiens in Paris his masterpiece, *Don Pasquale*. Two years later he was stricken with paralysis, became insane and in 1847 mercifully died and was buried in his native town of Bergamo—a victim, if ever there was one, of overwork.

In view of Donizetti's methods it is hardly surprising that much of his music sounds very superficial nowadays. Nevertheless there is nearly always something worth listening to even in the "serious" operas, which have suffered especially from the assaults of time; after a succession of banalities we are suddenly confronted with a page or two of high inspiration. This is particularly true of *Lucia di Lammermoor* wherein both the quantity and the quality of inspiration are exceptionally abundant. It is difficult for us today to appreciate the subtlety of the famous Mad Scene but its effect on contemporaries can be measured by the fact that it reduced audiences to tears. Much of the love music is highly plastic and moving, and it would be difficult to overpraise the mastery of the famous sextet, possibly the best example of concerted vocal music in Italian opera up to that time. Modern denigrators may be reminded that Tolstoy in *Anna Karenina* and Flaubert in *Madame Bovary* both chose *Lucia* as an example of great sentimental opera.

Still there is no doubt that of all his operas *Don Pasquale* represents Donizetti's attributes as a composer in their most favourable light. The melodies are as distinctive as they are spontaneous; the orchestration is skilful, the technical mastery of composition admirable. The fusion of words and music could hardly be better, and the rapid movement and the high spirits of the whole delight us today as much as ever. *Don Pasquale* is the final example of the genuine *opera buffa* school of Cimarosa and Goldoni, the last and most luscious fruit of that delightful tree. It seems incredible that it should have been written on the verge of a complete nervous collapse.

VII

THE SIMPLICITY OF GENIUS

GIUSEPPE VERDI, the outstanding figure among all Italian operatic composers, was born in the autumn of 1813 in a hamlet outside the little town of Busseto in the Duchy of Parma. Of peasant stock, he experienced the very real rigours of peasant childhood, and himself was not ashamed to proclaim that all his lifetime he remained a peasant at heart. The fact is of importance because it was not a little due to this hard, stubborn, peasant-like trait in his character that he was able to effect the revolution in Italian opera associated with his name.

Though as a boy uncommonly susceptible to music, he seems to have possessed little of the facility and none of the precocity characteristic of so many Italian composers; he began by writing some decidedly poor music for the local military band and the local church, as well as a number of rather commonplace songs. When, thanks to the discriminating generosity of a prosperous Busseto shopkeeper, he was enabled to go to Milan to study he failed to gain admittance to the Conservatoire. Emphatically Verdi belonged, not unlike Wagner, to the race of composers who achieve mastery only by the sweat of their brow and the strength of their determination.

After his rebuff at the Conservatoire young Verdi was fortunate enough to find a competent teacher who also proved himself a useful friend, and eventually he was given the opportunity to write an opera, *Oberto*, produced a few years later (1839) at La Scala. Though comparatively undistinguished, it achieved sufficient success to get him a contract to write another opera, equally unimportant save for the fact that it nearly caused Verdi to abandon operatic composition altogether. For this, a comic opera, coincided for Verdi with a period of great grief which seems to have stunned him. His beloved young wife, the daughter of his Busseto benefactor, had died two years before, leaving him two children who in their turn died, one after the other, during the actual period of its composition. In the circumstances it is scarcely surprising that *Il Finto Stanislao* was not a success.

To the wise forbearance of the impresario Merelli the world owes the renewed activity of one of its three greatest operatic composers. By a friendly stratagem he persuaded the reluctant Verdi to read an opera libretto which Nicolai had failed to set to music. As he read, almost in spite of himself, Verdi became more and more enthusiastic—and thus was born the opera *Nabucco*, destined to win spectacular success with critics and public alike. Its production at La Scala in 1842 marked the real foundation of Verdi's operatic career. His debt to Rossini and to the technical procedure of Donizetti was still obvious, but this music possessed a new flavour, a strength of emotion, a complete sincerity and a genuine patriotic fervour that found an immediate response in the hearts of his audience. Henceforward Verdi was to be indissolubly linked with the political aspirations of the Risorgimento; his operas became symbols of revolt against the Austrian domination and a recurrent excuse for patriotic demonstrations, though several of them, such as *I Lombardi* (1843), *Attila* (1846), *La Battaglia di Legnano* (1849), also possessed in varying degree pure musical merit. Equally potent was the patriotic appeal of *Ernani* and *Macbeth*, but here the musical interest remains transcendent.

Ernani is rarely heard nowadays, but so discerning a critic as Bernard Shaw considered that the uncompromising sincerity of the music definitely added nobility to the play of Victor Hugo's on which the opera is based. *Macbeth*, revived on several occasions in recent years, is still able to impress us with its sombre, intense dramatic power shown above all in the magnificent choruses of the last act. It is the most interesting of all Verdi's early operas and was moreover his especial favourite; as a mark of gratitude he dedicated it to his benefactor, the father of his dead wife, and he found it good enough

GIUSEPPE VERDI
Painting by Giovanni Boldini, 1886

eighteen years later, in 1865, to be worthy of revision and production at the Paris Opera—the only version of the opera now available to the public. Yet one other opera dating from the preparative period of Verdi's development should be mentioned: *Luisa Miller* (1849), his first experiment in what may be called intimate expression, a kind of precursor of *La Traviata*. Indeed there is much tender and moving music in *Luisa Miller*, which has latterly been revived in Germany and Italy.

The success of these operas placed Verdi unquestionably ahead of his contemporaries and immediate predecessors such as Mercadante. With a view to conducting and producing *I Masnadieri* he was invited in 1847 to London where the English critics thought little of this opera and of his music in general. He must already have made a good deal of money because it was at this time that he bought the farm of S. Agata which, progressively enlarged and improved, was destined to play such a beneficent and integral part in his life. From now onwards Verdi betook himself to the country whenever he could, became a practical farmer and, most important of all, laid the foundations of that robust vitality which, in extreme old age, enabled him to work the miracles of *Otello* and *Falstaff*.

There immediately followed the three operas by which Verdi is still best known to the public at large: *Rigoletto* (1851), *Il Trovatore* and *La Traviata* (both 1853). The music of all three remains so familiar that no detailed appraisement seems necessary. Mention however should be made of the great difficulty experienced by Verdi and his librettist, Piave, in getting *Rigoletto* past the Venetian censorship. Not only was the subject itself considered horrible and crude, but Victor Hugo's *Le Roi s'amuse*, the original source of the libretto, was deemed dangerous and revolutionary; only by changing the locale and all the names could there be any question of its being licensed at all. Here we see clearly the difference between Verdi and his predecessors; he dug his toes in, absolutely refusing to change a note of the music, threatening to withdraw the opera altogether. He always considered it one of his best works—and, like Stravinsky, I agree with him.

The magnificent tunes of *Il Trovatore* immediately captured the hearts of the Roman public who first heard it, as they have held the hearts of the world public ever since. Perhaps it would not be inapposite to describe *Il Trovatore* as the apotheosis of democratic qualities in music; for it is not refined and certainly not intellectual.

La Traviata, on the other hand, was a definite failure on its first production in Venice; the public apparently found difficulty in appreciating the novel intimacy of this music. Success however, not only in Italy but in Europe at large, was not long in coming, though in the first instance at any rate it was something of a *succès de scandale*. *La Traviata* was viewed as highly erotic and immoral, an apology for illicit love and an attack on the institution of marriage. Needless to say the English critics were particularly emphatic in this opinion.

The operas of the next sixteen years may be regarded as products of a transitional period. Nearly all of them are of interest. Two were definitely written for, and produced in, Paris to French librettos: *I Vespri Siciliani* (1855) and *Don Carlos* (1867). These French commissions attest the high place to which Verdi had then attained, because up till 1870 Paris, not Vienna or Milan, remained the Mecca of the operatic world. In *I Vespri Siciliani* may be noted the first traces of a Meyerbeerian influence still more evident in *Don Carlos*. Neither opera can be regarded as completely success-

VERDI'S 'RIGOLETTO'
Lithographed music cover by M. and N. Hanhart after J. Brandard, c. 1855

ful, though in *Don Carlos* there is some magnificent music, the granite-like duet between the Grand Inquisitor and King Philip being one of the master-pieces of all operatic literature. But the big auto-da-fé scene is, for Verdi, strangely ineffective and the great length of the opera—which the composer himself, not altogether felicitously, tried to reduce in a revised version (1884) —remains a grievous handicap.

Simon Boccanegra (1857), with much fine sombre music and a well-nigh unintelligible plot, is of primary interest as marking the first operatic collab-oration between Boito and Verdi, in 1881, for the production of a revised version. It has frequently been revived in recent years with the success that the nobility of the music certainly deserves. *Un Ballo in Maschera* (1859) has always ranked in popularity just below the favourites among Verdi's operas. Nevertheless it is equally important because here, in addition to admirable characterization and much highly expressive music, we catch in the light-

VERDI'S 'I MASNADIERI'
Jenny Lind and Lablache at Her Majesty's Theatre, London, 1847

heartedness of the page Oscar and in the sarcastic humour of the men's chorus at the end of the second act a glimpse of that plant which, budding again in the music of Fra Melitone in *La Forza del Destino*, burst into full bloom in *Falstaff*. It was during the alarums and excursions attendant on his fight with the Neapolitan censorship over Scribe's libretto—*Un Ballo in Maschera* was originally *Gustave III*, a play dealing with the famous King of Sweden—that Verdi became so to say officially linked with the movement for Italian unity. For all over the walls of Naples was scrawled "Viva VERDI", which everybody knew to be an acrostic for "Viva Emanuele, Re d'Italia". Though a prime favourite of mine, *La Forza del Destino*, produced (1862) in St. Petersburg, of all unlikely places, and revised (1869) for Milan, can scarcely be considered significant in Verdi's development; its attraction lies in its wealth of beautiful and wholly characteristic melodies.

Whether *Aida* (1871) is to be regarded as the culmination of this period or the beginning of the next is still disputed. In either case it is a masterpiece, written, as everybody knows, for the Cairo festivities in connection with the opening of the Suez Canal. It has been occasionally belittled as an

VERDI'S 'IL TROVATORE'
Engraved title-page of piano score, c. 1854

essentially *ad hoc* opera. Nothing could be more erroneous; for a long while Verdi refused the Khedive's commission and it was not till he read and almost fell in love with the scenario that he consented to write the music. He took immense pains both with this and the conversion of the scenario into a regular libretto with the results familiar to everybody. There is no call to praise the technical mastery of *Aida* or any detail of it, but it may be asserted with some confidence that the blend of pictorial and emotional atmosphere in the third act ranks among the highlights of European music.

Nobody would have been more surprised than Verdi himself had he been told after *Aida* that his two greatest operas still lay in the future. Probably at that time, certainly after the composition three years later of the Manzoni Requiem Mass, he seems to have thought that his professional career was over. For a long time past politics and farming had begun to occupy a progressively more important part in his life. With his then particular crony, the conductor Mariani, he indulged in some gun-running for Garibaldi; he was persuaded by his idol Cavour to sit unhappily as a Deputy in the newly constituted Italian Chamber; he married his beloved companion Giuseppina and spent most of the year at S. Agata, where every morning before breakfast he inspected his crops and his horses, the breeding of which he made something of a speciality.

How and why he was eventually persuaded to write *Otello* is not altogether clear though obviously the influence and new-born admiration of Boito counted for much. This very remarkable man, who had already composed the famous opera *Mefistofele*, appears deliberately to have sacrificed his own music to the provision for Verdi of the two best librettos in the annals of Italian opera: *Otello* and *Falstaff*. The former was produced in 1886, the latter in 1893, with several years of work behind each of them. Both are miracles. The technical mastery of *Falstaff* has never been surpassed and the mellow humour and the sparkle of it, the tender treatment of the young lovers, the ethereal music of the fairies, seem scarcely credible when we consider the eighty years of their begetter. But is not *Otello* in reality less credible still? For this, the greatest of all Italian tragic operas, in a sense the climax of every national and typically Italian characteristic, the very quintessence of passionate emotion, strong, terrible, heart-breaking and wistful by turns, was written by an old man of seventy-three. Many of us feel that in the last act Verdi and Boito actually improved upon Shakespeare; if so, no more need be said.

In 1901, eight years after the production of *Falstaff*, Verdi died, a Senator of the Kingdom of Italy, himself the sovereign and the very embodiment of his country's music, a national hero if ever there was one.

Perhaps the outstanding historic importance of Verdi is that he definitely put an end to the old semi-improvised opera; sometimes he wrote rapidly, sometimes slowly, but he always took uncommon pains in the matter of characterization and of interpreting, orchestrally and vocally, the dramatic situation as faithfully as he could. He succeeded, thanks to his iron will, in abolishing the previous tyranny of interpreters, especially singer-interpreters; for him the composer had a right to reign supreme. Nevertheless there is more to Verdi even than all this. He was a great if in a sense a limited man, and his greatness lay precisely in those qualities of sincerity and simplicity which, as many a musician must have noticed, often make his music sound so much more effective in performance than on paper. Many lesser men have possessed better taste; no man has ever had a larger measure of musical integrity. Boito said that of all the great composers he had known, Wagner, Rossini and Meyerbeer included, Verdi was the one who interested him the most. He may well have been justified, for there is nothing more fascinating than the great simplicity of great genius.

CARUSO AND SEMBRICH IN PUCCINI'S 'LA BOHÈME'
German drawing, c. 1900

VIII

'A HUNTER OF WILD DUCK AND LIBRETTI'

IT is not generally realized how sparse has been the production of successful operas in Italy since Verdi's death. Let us take the most recent composers first. Respighi, Casella and Malipiero, though men of recognized international position, cannot truthfully be said between them to have written a single opera that has achieved a permanent place in the national, much less the international, repertory. The youngest, Dallapiccola (b. 1904), is much esteemed and has written at least one opera (*Il Prigioniero*) which has been produced both in Italy and in the United States. He is however a disciple of atonality and therefore perforce appeals only to a limited public. Undoubtedly the most successful has been Ildebrando Pizzetti (b. 1880) whose best-known opera, *Debora e Jaele*, was produced in Milan in 1923. He still writes operas with some regularity—*Vanna Lupa* and the decidedly attractive one-act *Ifigenia* are the most recent—admired perhaps rather than loved in his own country but little known abroad. Pizzetti is a master of the continuous recitative in which, unlike Richard Strauss, he succeeds in keeping the voices audible, never allowing them to be completely overwhelmed by the orchestra. He writes with great distinction for the chorus also.

When we come to the so-called realist school, usually considered post-Verdian, the reader may be astonished to find how many of these operas were in fact written before Verdi's death. Catalani, sometimes described as the most promising of Verdi's successors, was not a realist at all; moreover he had already produced his outstanding opera, *La Wally*, in 1892—one year before his premature death at the age of thirty-nine. Ponchielli's *La Gioconda* was produced in 1876; of the three operas by which Giordano is now remembered only one, *Siberia*, dates from the twentieth century, while the other two, *Andrea Chénier*, probably his best work, and *Fedora* (the opera which first had the distinction of introducing a bicycle on to the lyric stage), were produced in 1896 and 1898 respectively. Cilea was already thirty-six when in 1902 he produced his charming and unpretentious *Adriana Lecouvreur*, which is lyric rather than realist in character.

It is often forgotten too that those hardy twins, "Cav. and Pag.", antedate Verdi's death, "Cav." by eleven and "Pag." by nine years. Not only force of circumstances, but the alleged resemblance of their authors as having during their long careers achieved only one successful opera apiece, seems to have linked them together indissolubly. This however is not quite fair because whereas Leoncavallo (1858–1919), the composer of *I Pagliacci*, never did in fact produce anything else of moment, Mascagni (1863–1945) can be credited with at least two other operas of importance besides *Cavalleria Rusticana*: *L'Amico Fritz* and *Iris*. Neither of course has attained equal popularity but one act at any rate of *Iris* is wholly excellent and there is much charming music in *L'Amico Fritz*. Both, moreover, still have their places in the current Italian repertory. But these, too, were written before the turn of the century, in 1891 and 1898; and, to round off this aspect of the matter, it may be noted that even among Puccini's operas *Manon Lescaut*, *La Bohème* and *Tosca* were all written before 1901.

Musicians as a body are not enamoured of Giacomo Puccini but the fact is that of all contemporary operatic composers, with the exception of Richard Strauss, he alone has established himself permanently—and with indubitably greater success than Strauss—in the international repertory. The fact may be unpalatable; it remains a fact.

Puccini was born at Lucca in 1858 of a distinguished family of musicians and had the sense to realize very early in life—in fact immediately after his

PIETRO MASCAGNI
Caricature by Caran d'Ache, c. 1902

famous walk from Lucca to Pisa to hear *Aida*—that he should write only for the theatre. Of his first two operas, *Le Villi* (1884) and *Edgar* (1889), the former was a success, the latter a failure; it was not till 1893 that there appeared the opera destined to lay the foundation of his international fame: *Manon Lescaut*. Comparison of this work with the more famous *Manon* of Massenet is ineluctable. Massenet's opera has the advantage of a better libretto, and greater elegance and taste, but there is in Puccini's *Manon* a spontaneous profusion of musical ideas, a freshness, a youthful vitality not to be matched in the Frenchman's score.

Puccini, never a rapid worker, took three years to complete and produce *La Bohème* (1896). Since this remains probably the most popular opera in the world little need be said about it, but people may usefully be reminded that its idiom was new enough to perplex the original audience. As an example of theatrical effectiveness the score would be difficult to surpass, and I cannot pretend to resist, or even to wish to resist, its superlative charm. In 1900 there followed *Tosca*, which Puccini later came definitely to dislike. Perhaps from the aesthetic point of view he was right, but there is in it some fine music, the announcement of the victory of Marengo for instance

'RIDI, PAGLIACCIO!'
Autograph inscription by Ruggiero Leoncavallo

in the second act and the luscious, tender love duet in the last. *Madame Butterfly*, now the runner-up to *La Bohème* in popularity, was hissed off the stage on its first appearance in 1904. In its technical and experimental aspect it shows distinct progress, but it scarcely possesses the unity of its two predecessors, achieving neither the charm of the one nor the stark effectiveness of the other.

With the eventual triumph of *Madame Butterfly* Puccini reached the pinnacle of operatic fame. In 1910 *La Fanciulla del West*, commissioned by the Metropolitan Opera House, was produced in New York with what appeared to be, but was not, complete success. The remarkable thing about this conventional Western melodrama, wherein whisky flows like water, is that it contains as much good music as it does. The not infrequent designation of it as a pot-boiler is preposterous; Puccini, who made a habit of falling in love with his heroines, developed an admiration for Minnie only second to that he felt for Cio-Cio-San and Mimi. The three one-act operas known in Italy as *Il Trittico* appeared in 1918. Not improbably they mark the summit of Puccini's achievement; the brutal realism of *Il Tabarro*, the mystic sentiment of *Suor Angelica* (Puccini's especial favourite) and the sly, brilliant humour of *Gianni Schicchi*, are certainly worthy of the highest admiration, yet *Il Trittico* as an entity has never won the place in the operatic repertory deserved by its merits. Much the same may be said of *Turandot*, which

Puccini did not live to finish. Many have thought that this opera denotes a new stage in Puccini's development and might well have been followed by a great masterpiece. Skilfully completed by Alfano, *Turandot* was produced in 1926, eighteen months after Puccini's death.

To regard Puccini as a mere seeker after popularity and money is wholly unjustified. He took immense pains with his music and achieved a mastery of the orchestra all his own. He took even greater pains in the discovery and fashioning of librettos, of which he discarded many more than he ever set to music. Indeed he once amusingly described himself as "a passionate hunter . . . of wild duck and of opera libretti". In no sense a great man, he remains a consummate musician. He also remains the last of a long line of paramount Italian composers of opera. Whether or not he will eventually find a successor time alone can show. The omens are not propitious because, a little owing to the decadence of singing, a little to the growing rivalry of other attractions, most of all to economic conditions, the whole future of the operatic form, even in Italy, seems in jeopardy.

GIACOMO PUCCINI
Autograph letter signed with a self-caricature

INDEX

(The figures in italics refer to pages on which illustrations appear)